25 Projects for ART Explorers

25 Projects for ART Explorers

CHRISTINE M. KIRKER

ALA Editions

CHICAGO 2018

Christine M. Kirker is a library associate with the Carroll County (Maryland) Public Library. Since joining the library staff in 2005, Christine has developed and presented many programs for children of all ages, including monthly preschool science programs. Previously, Christine spent ten years at the University of Maryland, Baltimore County (UMBC) as a research analyst for the Office of Institutional Research.

© 2018 by the American Library Association

Extensive effort has gone into ensuring the reliability of the information in this book; however, the publisher makes no warranty, express or implied, with respect to the material contained herein.

ISBN: 978-0-8389-1739-8 (paper)

Library of Congress Cataloging-in-Publication Data
Names: Kirker, Christine, author.
Title: 25 projects for art explorers / Christine M. Kirker.
Other titles: Twenty five projects for art explorers
Description: Chicago : ALA Editions, An imprint of the American Library
  Association, 2018. | Includes bibliographical references and index.
Identifiers: LCCN 2018010854 | ISBN 9780838917398 (print : alk. paper)
Subjects: LCSH: Art—Study and teaching (Elementary) | Children's literature,
  American.
Classification: LCC N350 .K515 2018 | DDC 707.1—dc23
LC record available at https://lccn.loc.gov/2018010854

Book design by Kimberly Thornton in the Vista and Cardea typefaces.

⊚ This paper meets the requirements of ANSI/NISO Z39.48-1992 (Permanence of Paper).

Printed in the United States of America
22 21 20 19 18   5 4 3 2 1

To my family, who supports and encourages me to
explore the beauty in our world. —CMK

"Every child is an artist. The problem is how to remain
an artist once he grows up." —Pablo Picasso

contents

introduction

With the emphasis on incorporating STEM activities (science, technology, engineering, and mathematics) for children at young ages, art is often neglected. Schools are forced to meet curriculum goals with standardized testing beginning at young ages, leaving little time for creativity. With clear text and inventive activities, *25 Projects for Art Explorers* will spark children's interest in art and encourage creativity, collaboration, and critical thinking. It will introduce children to a variety of art techniques, each presented through the lens of a representative picture book. Children will see the technique in the published book and then create their own masterpiece using the detailed directions that follow. Full of information and imagination, *25 Projects for Art Explorers* will reinforce learning, encourage experimentation, and build an appreciation for art and the creative process.

1

Inside Outside

Inside Outside

Lizi Boyd. San Francisco, CA: Chronicle Books, 2013.

In this wordless book, Lizi Boyd follows a boy through a year of activities, both indoors and out. Die cuts on each "inside" page offer a glimpse to the outside world, while "outside" pages allow readers to peek inside. *Inside Outside* encourages the use of imagination and storytelling.

ABOUT THE ILLUSTRATOR:
Lizi Boyd

Lizi Boyd is best known for her wordless children's picture books. She enjoys trying new papers and surfaces to create her art, along with new artistic techniques. In order to find the perfect paper to enhance her paintings, Boyd will often create the same illustration on multiple papers while discovering which paper works best. You can learn more about Lizi Boyd and see images of her work at liziboyd.com.

ABOUT THE TECHNIQUE: Gouache

Gouache paint is similar to watercolor paint, although the color is opaque, or not able to be seen through, unlike watercolor, which is transparent.

BOOKS TO DISPLAY

Big Bear Little Chair by Lizi Boyd. San Francisco, CA: Chronicle Books, 2015.

Flashlight by Lizi Boyd. San Francisco, CA: Chronicle Books, 2014.

I Love Grandma by Lizi Boyd. Cambridge, MA: Candlewick Press, 2009.

Programming Tip

Flashlight by Lizi Boyd is a fun way to explore the dark. Have children retell this wordless story, imagining the sounds the creatures are making through the night.

Art Project: Inside Outside Book

Think about your favorite season and some of the things you may see inside and outside. Create an inside page with a cut window opening to the outside page.

PIECES NEEDED
- Brown paper grocery bags cut to the size desired (each child will need two pieces)
- Pencil
- Scissors
- Gouache paints
- Paintbrushes and plate for paint palette
- Water and paper towels for rinsing brushes
- Table covers to protect tables as needed
- Stapler

DIRECTIONS
1. Create your inside page. What are some things you may see inside? Draw the details of your inside page. Mark where you will place your window.
2. Cut the window opening for the inside page. Place the outside page underneath the inside page and mark the spot where the window will feature an outside item. The window should open to a special element on the outside page.
3. Draw the details of your outside page.
4. Use gouache paint in a variety of colors to enhance the illustrations. Allow the paint to dry before adding additional details and color.
5. After both pages are dry, staple the inside page on top of the outside page in the upper left corner.
6. Sign your work of art and display!

2
The Easter Egg
Watercolor and Gouache

The Easter Egg

Jan Brett. New York: G. P. Putnam's Sons, 2010.
Hoppi the bunny is excited to decorate his
first-ever Easter egg, and he hopes to win the
chance to help the Easter Rabbit hide eggs on
Easter morning. While Hoppi is trying to choose
the best way to decorate his egg, he discovers a
robin's egg that has fallen from the nest. Hoppi
has to decide whether to decorate his egg or help
Mother Robin.

ABOUT THE ILLUSTRATOR: Jan Brett

Jan Brett is best known for her children's books. Her books feature intricate bor-
ders that tell their own story or foretell future action. Jan Brett travels around the
world to gain authenticity and inspiration for her books, researching the location,
architecture, animals, and clothing of the area. You can learn more about Jan Brett
and see images of her work at janbrett.com.

Programming Tip

Jan Brett has a wide variety of books that cover
every season and holiday,
as well as many folktales.
In addition, her website
has an extensive list of
activities for each of her
books. Make use of this
wonderful resource when
planning activities for
children (**janbrett.com/
activities_pages.htm**).

ABOUT THE TECHNIQUE:
Watercolor and Gouache

Watercolor is a type of paint mixed with water.
Gouache paint is similar to watercolor paint,
although the color is opaque, or not able to
be seen through, unlike watercolor, which is
transparent. Jan Brett uses both watercolor
and gouache to bring to life her intricate illustrations.

BOOKS TO DISPLAY

Gingerbread Christmas by Jan Brett. New
York: G. P. Putnam's Sons, 2016.

The Mermaid by Jan Brett. New York: G. P.
Putnam's Sons, 2017.

The Turnip by Jan Brett. New York: G. P.
Putnam's Sons, 2015.

Art Project: Decorated Eggs

Decorating eggs is a symbol of spring and rebirth that has been shared by many cultures for thousands of years. Using watercolor and gouache paints, create a brightly decorated egg that celebrates spring.

PIECES NEEDED

- Egg shape copied onto watercolor or regular copy paper
- Watercolor and gouache paints
- Paintbrushes and plate for paint palette
- Water and paper towels for rinsing brushes
- Table covers to protect tables as needed

DIRECTIONS

1. Using Jan Brett's egg template, copy the image onto watercolor paper or regular copy paper (janbrett.com/mural_easter_egg/easter_egg_mural _a_design_egg.htm).
2. Using watercolor and gouache paints, add color to your egg. Remember the more water you add, the lighter the paint will be. If you want to add another layer of paint over an already painted area, make sure it is dry first.
3. Sign your work of art and display!

3

"Slowly, Slowly, Slowly," said the Sloth

"Slowly, Slowly, Slowly," Said the Sloth

Eric Carle. New York: Philomel Books, 2002.

Eric Carle creates the exotic beauty of the Amazon rain forest with painted tissue paper. While the other animals are moving quickly through their day, the Sloth is moving slowly. After being questioned about his characteristics throughout the book, the Sloth finally reveals his secret of a leisurely life.

ABOUT THE ILLUSTRATOR: Eric Carle

Eric Carle is best known for his painted tissue paper collage children's books, which include *The Very Hungry Caterpillar*. His illustrations incorporate bright colors and simple designs. In 2003, he received the Laura Ingalls Wilder Award for his contribution to American children's literature. You can learn more about Eric Carle and see images of his work at eric-carle.com/home.html.

Programming Tip

Eric Carle has an assortment of reader-contributed activities listed on his website to go with many of his books. Make use of this wonderful resource when planning activities for children (eric-carle.com/catexchange.html).

ABOUT THE TECHNIQUE: Painted Tissue Paper

Beginning with white tissue paper, Eric Carle hand paints the papers in a variety of colors and prints, then cuts and layers them to form his illustrations. Detailed instructions for creating painted tissue paper and a video of the process are available at eric-carle.com/creativeprojects.html.

BOOKS TO DISPLAY

Baby Bear, Baby Bear, What Do You See? by Eric Carle. New York: Henry Holt, 2007.

Mister Seahorse by Eric Carle. New York: Philomel Books, 2004.

The Mixed-Up Chameleon by Eric Carle. New York: Crowell, 1984.

Art Project: Painted Tissue Paper Collage

Create your own jungle scene with a sloth! Paint tissue paper with your own unique patterns, then cut shapes and glue to the sloth image to make your own collage.

PIECES NEEDED

- Copies of sloth image (provided)
- White tissue paper
- Glue
- Scissors
- Watercolor paints
- Paintbrushes and plate for paint palette
- Water and paper towels for rinsing brushes
- Table covers to protect tables as needed

DIRECTIONS

1. Paint white tissue paper with vibrant colors and patterns as is demonstrated on Eric Carle's resource website (eric-carle.com/creativeprojects.html).
2. When the tissue paper is dry, trace the sloth image and begin cutting shapes to glue on the sloth picture. Use a variety of colors and patterns to add depth and dimension to your picture.
3. Add painted tissue paper to create the jungle background.
4. Sign your work of art and display!

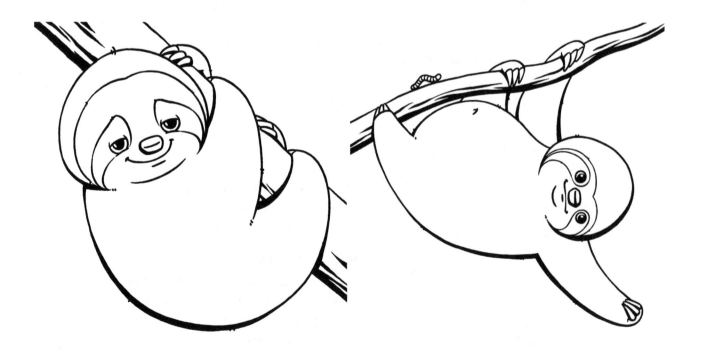

4

Trombone Shorty

Watercolor Collage

Trombone Shorty

Troy Andrews. New York: Abrams Books for Young Readers, 2015.

Trombone Shorty shares the story of how legendary jazz artist Troy Andrews gained his nickname and his fame. Andrews grew up in New Orleans, surrounded by the rich sounds of music. By the time he was six, he was leading his own band and playing a trombone twice as long as he was. Bold illustrations by Bryan Collier bring to life the sounds and the passion of Troy Andrews and his vibrant city!

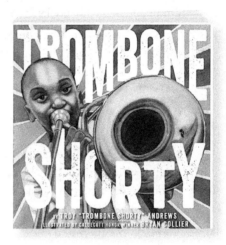

ABOUT THE ILLUSTRATOR: Bryan Collier

Bryan Collier is best known for his painting style that combines watercolors and collage in his children's books. Collier is the recipient of the Coretta Scott King Award and the Caldecott Honor award for *Trombone Shorty* (2016). He also received Caldecott Honor awards for *Dave the Potter: Artist, Poet, Slave* (2010), *Rosa* (2005), and *Martin's Big Words: The Life of Martin Luther King Jr.* (2001). Collier started working with watercolors and photo collage when he was fifteen. While in high school, he won first place in a congressional competition, allowing him to display his painting in the Capitol in Washington, D.C., for one year. You can learn more about Bryan Collier and see images of his work at bryancollier.com/index.php.

ABOUT THE TECHNIQUE: Watercolor Collage

Watercolor collage combines watercolor

Programming Tip

My Country, 'Tis of Thee: How One Song Reveals the History of Civil Rights by Claire Rudolf Murphy explains the history of the song "America." Share this book during Black History Month or for another American history or holiday program. Create a watercolor collage American flag or other historic image to accompany this theme.

painting with collaged items to enhance the picture created. Watercolor is a type of paint mixed with water. Collage is a technique of composing a work of art by attaching pieces of different materials (such as paper, cloth, or wood) to a single surface.

BOOKS TO DISPLAY

City Shapes by Diana Murray, illustrated by Bryan Collier. New York: Little, Brown, 2016.

I, Too, Am America by Langston Hughes, illustrated by Bryan Collier. New York: Simon and Schuster Books for Young Readers, 2012.

My Country, 'Tis of Thee: How One Song Reveals the History of Civil Rights by Claire Rudolf Murphy, illustrated by Bryan Collier. New York: Henry Holt, 2014.

Art Project: Watercolor Collage

Using the drawing available or a design of your choice, create a watercolor collage. Lightly paint with watercolors and add an assortment of collage items to finish the design. Collage ideas include music note stickers, strings from a guitar or violin, and scraps of sheet music.

PIECES NEEDED

- An assortment of images copied on watercolor paper. A suggestion to get started is provided.
- A variety of items to enhance the painting (musical notes, gems, ticket stubs, newspapers, collage paper, string, sheet music, etc.)
- Glue
- Scissors
- Watercolor paints
- Paintbrushes and plate for paint palette
- Water and paper towels for rinsing brushes
- Table covers to protect tables as needed

DIRECTIONS

1. Decide which picture you would like to create and have enough copies for each student. If you have watercolor paper available, use that to make the copies of the picture.
2. Add watercolors to the picture. The brush should not be too wet; you can always add more color if needed.
3. Choose collage pieces to glue to the picture to enhance the design. Use a variety of items to add depth and dimension to your picture.
4. Sign your work of art and display!

5
Hooray for Birds!

Hooray for Birds!

Lucy Cousins. Somerville, MA: Candlewick Press, 2017.

This interactive book is perfect to share with a group. Simple text and bold illustrations invite you to act like the birds described and then settle in your nest. Whether you are swooping, flapping, or flying, *Hooray for Birds!* is fun for all.

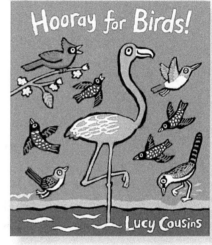

ABOUT THE ILLUSTRATOR: Lucy Cousins

Lucy Cousins is best known for her children's books, which include her Maisy series of picture books. After deciding to become a children's book illustrator, she experimented with drawing many animals until she decided that Maisy Mouse was her main character. You can learn more about Lucy Cousins and see images of her work at maisyfunclub.com.

Programming Tip

Lucy Cousins has a wide variety of Maisy books available that cover many life events and adventures. Visit Maisy's Fun Club to find games, coloring pages, and other activities (**maisyfunclub.com**).

ABOUT THE TECHNIQUE: Gouache

Gouache paint is similar to watercolor paint, although the color is opaque, or not able to be seen through, unlike watercolor, which is transparent. Lucy Cousins thickly outlines her illustrations with black paint first and then fills them with color.

BOOKS TO DISPLAY

Hooray for Fish! by Lucy Cousins. Cambridge, MA: Candlewick Press, 2005.

Jazzy in the Jungle by Lucy Cousins. Cambridge, MA: Candlewick Press, 2013.

Maisy Goes to the Local Bookstore by Lucy Cousins. Somerville, MA: Candlewick Press, 2017.

Art Project: Gouache Owl

Using the owl image provided or a bird created from your imagination, create your own boldly painted feathered friend. Try Lucy Cousins's technique of outlining the bird with a thick black line, allowing it to dry, then adding color.

PIECES NEEDED
- Owl copied onto watercolor paper, or a bird shape drawn
- Pencil
- Gouache paints
- Paintbrushes and plate for paint palette
- Water and paper towels for rinsing brushes
- Table covers to protect tables as needed

DIRECTIONS
1. If using the owl picture provided, make enough copies for each student, or have students draw a picture of a bird. If you have watercolor paper available, use that for the pictures copied and drawn.
2. Thickly outline the drawing with black paint, allowing it to dry after application.
3. Use gouache paint in a variety of bright colors for your bird. Allow the paint to dry before adding more details and color.
4. Sign your work of art and display!

6
Snowballs

Snowballs

Lois Ehlert. San Diego: Harcourt Brace, 1995.

Snowballs showcases a family of snow people created from random items saved throughout the year. This book features simple text making it a perfect winter tale to share with children of all ages. The photographs of items used throughout the book will inspire you to start your own collection so you are ready for the next snowfall.

ABOUT THE ILLUSTRATOR: Lois Ehlert

Lois Ehlert is best known for her children's books that feature bold colors and vibrant artwork. Ehlert is the recipient of the Caldecott Honor award for *Color Zoo* (1990). Ehlert's illustrations are created from vivid colored papers cut into the desired shapes along with objects she collects, such as seeds, leaves, shoelaces, and buttons. You can learn more about Lois Ehlert and see images of her work at loisehlert.weebly.com.

ABOUT THE TECHNIQUE: Cut Paper and Collage

Artwork made with cut paper and collage combines cut paper shapes with collaged items to enhance the picture created. The cut paper forms an outline for the base of the illustration. Collage is a technique of composing a work of art by attaching materials (such as paper, cloth, or wood) onto a single surface.

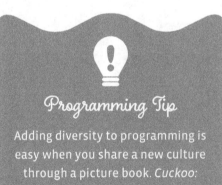

Programming Tip

Adding diversity to programming is easy when you share a new culture through a picture book. *Cuckoo: A Mexican Folktale* by Lois Ehlert (San Diego: Harcourt Brace, 1997) shares the traditional Mayan tale of how Cuckoo lost her feathers. The bilingual text and bold colors invite children to participate in the story. As an extension, use paper cutouts with paper fasteners to create a moving cuckoo to retell the story.

BOOKS TO DISPLAY

Color Zoo by Lois Ehlert. New York: Harper Festival, 1989.

Heart 2 Heart by Lois Ehlert. New York: Beach Lane Books, 2017.

Rrralph by Lois Ehlert. New York: Beach Lane Books, 2011.

Art Project: Snow Family Collage

Using premade "snowballs" in varying shapes and sizes, create a snow family adorned with a variety of collected materials.

PIECES NEEDED

- An assortment of white paper circles in various sizes
- White paper so participants can create additional details for any snow animals
- A variety of items to enhance the snow family (mittens, gloves, items found in nature, ribbons, string, tags, dried noodles, dried beans, colorful construction paper, etc.)
- Glue
- Scissors
- Table covers to protect tables as needed

DIRECTIONS

1. Begin by assembling the white paper circles to form your snow family.
2. If you are creating animals, cut additional shapes needed.
3. Use the items you have collected to create the details of the snow family. Use a variety of items and papers to add depth and dimension to your picture.
4. Sign your work of art and display!

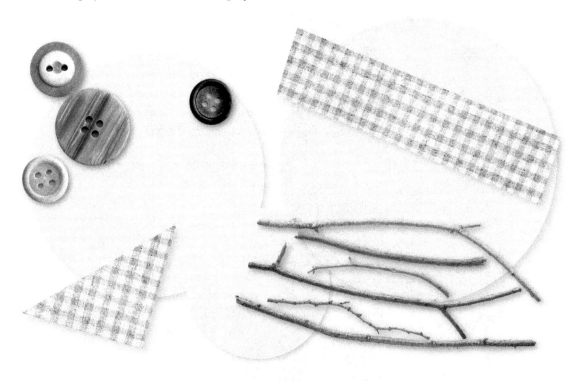

7

Go Away, Big Green Monster!

Go Away, Big Green Monster!

Ed Emberley. Boston: Little, Brown, 1992.
Ed Emberley's classic book empowers children to send the monster away. As the story unfolds, more of the monster is revealed on each page, until he is told to "Go Away." When the monster is dismissed, his features disappear page by page. By using die-cut paper, Emberley allows the reader to see how the monster is made with each new page.

ABOUT THE ILLUSTRATOR: Ed Emberley
Ed Emberley is best known for his children's book illustrations in which he often experiments with a variety of mixed media, including woodcuts, cut paper, pen and ink, and pencil. Many of his books have been written in collaboration with his wife, daughter, and son. Emberley is the recipient of the Caldecott Medal for best illustrated children's book, *Drummer Hoff* (1968), and the Caldecott Honor award for *One Wide River to Cross* (1967). You can learn more about Ed Emberley and experiment with many of his drawing techniques at edemberley.com/pages/main.aspx?section=home.

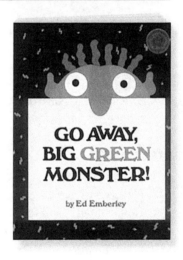

ABOUT THE TECHNIQUE: Cut Paper
Cut paper art uses shapes cut from papers and arranged into compositions. Papers are selected based on colors and patterns and can be painted with colors of your choosing.

! Programming Tip

Ed Emberley has an assortment of drawing books available to introduce drawing and art to people of all ages. For a fun activity, *Ed Emberley's Fingerprint Drawing Book* (New York: Little, Brown, 2000) provides simple step-by-step instructions for creating drawings using fingerprints and ink. Visit his website to explore his suggested activities (**edemberley.com/pages/main .aspx?section=activities**).

BOOKS TO DISPLAY

Spare Parts by Rebecca Emberley. New York: Roaring Brook Press, 2015.

Ten Little Beasties by Rebecca Emberley. New York: Roaring Brook Press, 2011.

There Was an Old Monster by Rebecca Emberley. New York: Orchard Books, 2009.

Art Project: Cut Paper Monsters

Monsters don't need to be scary. Once you create your own, you will see how fun they can be. Using a variety of cut shapes, make your own monster.

PIECES NEEDED

- An assortment of papers in a variety of patterns and colors
- Scissors
- Glue
- Large piece of construction paper to assemble your monster
- Table covers to protect tables as needed

DIRECTIONS

1. Think about what you want your monster to look like.
2. Cut paper to create your monster. The monster may need a head, eyes, a nose, ears, a mouth, and teeth. If you want to reinforce geometric shapes, use circles, squares, triangles, and rectangles for the monster's features.
3. Glue the items on a large piece of construction paper to create a monster.
4. Sign your work of art and display!

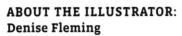

⑧

UnderGROUND

UnderGROUND

Denise Fleming. New York: Beach Lane Books, 2012.

UnderGROUND explores not only what we see at the surface but also what is actually happening underground. From worms to a rabbit den, discover the mysteries below. There is a whole world to explore underground, and Fleming's illustrations allow us to witness it.

ABOUT THE ILLUSTRATOR:
Denise Fleming

Denise Fleming is best known for her pulp paper illustrated children's books. Simple text accompanies her bold and unique illustrations, making her books accessible for children of all ages. Fleming is the recipient of the Caldecott Honor award for *In the Small, Small Pond* (1994). You can learn more about Denise Fleming, see images of her work, and find a variety of programming materials at denisefleming.com.

Programming Tip

Many of Denise Fleming's books explore the outside world through a child's eyes. After sharing *In the Tall, Tall Grass, In the Small, Small Pond,* or *UnderGROUND,* go outside and explore your local ecosystem. Take a magnifying glass, a pencil, and a notebook to write down and sketch pictures of what you discover.

ABOUT THE TECHNIQUE:
Pulp Papermaking

Pulp papermaking uses a fiber material mixed with water to create a slurry. Fleming uses cotton rag, but some prefer the simplicity of non-bleeding tissue paper. The wet fiber is poured through stencils onto a draining screen and then allowed to dry. This process creates an image set within the paper. You can learn more and watch a video demonstrating the process at denisefleming .com/pages/about/process/papermaking/ papermaking-main.html#gsc.tab=0.

BOOKS TO DISPLAY

5 Little Ducks by Denise Fleming. New York: Beach Lane Books, 2016.

In the Small, Small Pond by Denise Fleming. New York: Henry Holt, 1993.

Maggie and Michael Get Dressed by Denise Fleming. New York: Henry Holt, 2016.

Art Project: Tissue Paper Pulp Papermaking

Making your own pulp paper is fun and easy when you use this simplified method with non-bleeding tissue paper and a cookie cutter to create your design.

PIECES NEEDED

- Non-bleeding tissue paper
- Canvas, cut to 4 inches by 6 inches or your desired size (canvas often comes in 3-yard rolls)
- Corrugated cardboard
- Masking tape
- Cookie cutters
- Pencil
- Glue
- Bowls for water
- Paper towels
- Table covers to protect tables as needed

DIRECTIONS

1. Mount canvas to a piece of corrugated cardboard, using masking tape to secure the edges.
2. Lay a cookie cutter on the canvas. Trace the outline of the cookie cutter or leave the cookie cutter in place to pour your pulp in. If you trace the shape, place your pulp within the outline.
3. Working with one color at a time, tear tissue paper into small pieces, place the pieces in the bowl, and add enough water to wet the paper. Using your fingers, mix the water and paper, tearing and pressing pieces together to form pulpy paper. To create shading or tones of colors, mix two or more colors.
4. Press the wet tissue pulp onto the canvas image to start creating the paper.
5. Work one area at a time so that pieces overlap with each other. As the pulp dries, it will interlock and form a solid piece. Once a section is dry it cannot bond, so you may need to use a small amount of glue in order for wet pulp to bond to dry pulp.
6. Blot the paper pulp with paper towels to remove excess moisture.
7. Allow the pulp to dry and then remove from the canvas. Reuse the canvas for another project.
8. Sign your work of art and display!

9

My Garden

My Garden

Kevin Henkes. New York: Greenwillow Books, 2010.

A girl helps her mother tend a beautiful garden, while imagining what her own garden would be like. The carrots would definitely be invisible because she does not like carrots. If she picked a flower, it would grow back immediately, and the rabbits would all be made of delicious chocolate.

ABOUT THE ILLUSTRATOR:
Kevin Henkes

Kevin Henkes is best known for his children's picture books and novels. Henkes is the recipient of the Caldecott Medal for the best illustrated children's book, *Kitten's First Full Moon* (2005), and received Caldecott Honor awards for *Owen* (1994) and *Waiting* (2016). Henkes creates his illustrations in stages, first completing all the pencil sketches, then adding ink, and finally finishing with watercolor. You can learn more about Kevin Henkes, watch short videos of how he makes his books, and see images of his work at kevinhenkes.com.

ABOUT THE TECHNIQUE:
Ink and Watercolor

Watercolor is a type of paint mixed with water. By incorporating water, the paint colors can be diluted, creating lighter shades. Henkes often draws his illustrations in ink first and then adds watercolors.

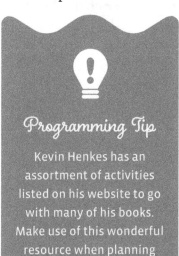

Programming Tip

Kevin Henkes has an assortment of activities listed on his website to go with many of his books. Make use of this wonderful resource when planning activities for children (kevinhenkes.com/for -teachers-librarians -parents).

BOOKS TO DISPLAY

Egg by Kevin Henkes. New York: Greenwillow Books, 2017.

Old Bear by Kevin Henkes. New York: Greenwillow Books, 2008.

Waiting by Kevin Henkes. New York: Greenwillow Books, 2015.

Art Project: In Your Garden

In the book *My Garden* by Kevin Henkes, a girl imagines all the wonderful things that would make her garden special. What would make your garden special? Would it have chocolate rabbits or strawberries that glow like lanterns? Maybe it would have rows of seashells. Practice sketching your garden, then add darker ink lines and watercolor.

PIECES NEEDED

- Light-colored watercolor paper or construction paper
- Pencil
- Black marker or ink pen
- Watercolor paints
- Paintbrushes and plate for paint palette
- Water and paper towels for rinsing brushes
- Table covers to protect tables as needed

DIRECTIONS

1. Using the pencil, sketch your garden.
2. Use black marker or ink to draw over the sketch.
3. Use watercolor paints to add color to the illustration. The brush should not be too wet; you can always add more color if needed.
4. Sign your work of art and display!

10

Snowman's Story

Mixed Media

Snowman's Story

Will Hillenbrand. New York: Two Lions, 2014.

When a snowman falls asleep after reading a story to his animal friends, the rabbit that's been hiding in the snowman's hat runs off with the book. The snowman and his friends chase the rabbit, only to discover that the book is best shared. Illustrations and the reader's imagination tell the story in this wordless book.

ABOUT THE ILLUSTRATOR: Will Hillenbrand

Will Hillenbrand is best known for his mixed media children's illustrated books, including his Bear and Mole series of picture books. He began drawing early, illustrating the exaggerated tales he heard from customers in his father's barbershop. You can learn more about Will Hillenbrand and see images of his work at willhillenbrand.com/index.html.

ABOUT THE TECHNIQUE: Mixed Media

Mixed media art is created by using more than one medium. Will Hillenbrand often uses graphite and colored pencils, chalk pastels, crayon, ink, watercolor, and collage in his illustrations.

BOOKS TO DISPLAY

All for a Dime! A Bear and Mole Story by Will Hillenbrand. New York: Holiday House, 2015.

Down by the Barn by Will Hillenbrand. New York: Two Lions, 2014.

Off We Go! A Bear and Mole Story by Will Hillenbrand. New York: Holiday House, 2013.

Programming Tip

Thumbprints are unique, just like you! Make your own thumbprint portrait (https://www.youtube.com/watch?v=zrHKHHxcqkc) and try a variety of other activities on Will Hillenbrand's website (**willhillenbrand.com/activities.html**).

Art Project:
Watercolor and Crayon Resist Winter Scene

Think about what you see outside on a winter day—how does the snow look on the trees or ground? Draw your winter scene in white crayon and then paint the scene with watercolor paints. The area you have drawn with the crayon will resist the paint, so your snow scene will stay white while the background has the colors of your choice.

PIECES NEEDED

- Watercolor paper or construction paper
- White crayon
- Watercolor paints
- Paintbrushes and plate for paint palette
- Water and paper towels for rinsing brushes
- Table covers to protect tables as needed

DIRECTIONS

1. Using a white crayon, draw a winter snow scene. Think about adding snow people, trees, or animals to your picture.
2. Using watercolor paints, paint the background colors of your winter scene—possibly a blue sky or gray clouds, or green peeking out of the grass or trees. The brush should not be too wet; you can always add more color if needed.
3. Sign your work of art and display!

11

Flying Frogs and Walking Fish

Torn and Cut Paper Collage

Flying Frogs and Walking Fish: Leaping Lemurs, Tumbling Toads, Jet-Propelled Jellyfish, and More Surprising Ways That Animals Move

Steve Jenkins and Robin Page. Boston: Houghton Mifflin Harcourt, 2016.

Flying Frogs and Walking Fish features animals that get around in surprising ways. Have you heard of a flying snake or a walking octopus? Jenkins and Page explore the unusual and extraordinary, fascinating children and adults alike with the familiar and unknown real world of animals.

ABOUT THE ILLUSTRATOR: Steve Jenkins

Steve Jenkins is best known for his collage-illustrated children's books. Jenkins is the recipient of the Caldecott Honor award for *What Do You Do with a Tail Like This?* (2003). Jenkins's books introduce us to science, biology, and the environment with collage illustrations and fascinating facts. You can learn more about Steve Jenkins, watch a short video of him making a book, and see images of his work at stevejenkinsbooks.com.

ABOUT THE TECHNIQUE: Torn and Cut Paper Collage

Collage is the technique of composing a work of art by attaching various materials not normally associated with one another on a single surface. Jenkins first creates pencil sketches of his illustrations to use as templates for

Programming Tip

If working with younger children, select one or two animal shapes and create precut collage packages for each child. Include an animal and various papers already cut to fit the animal. The children will learn the technique of collage work without becoming frustrated by trying to cut exact animal body parts. In addition, collage paper will not be wasted.

cutting out the pieces of paper he will use for his collage. He uses paper in a variety of colors and textures for his final product.

BOOKS TO DISPLAY

Actual Size by Steve Jenkins. Boston: Houghton Mifflin, 2004.

The Beetle Book by Steve Jenkins. Boston: Houghton Mifflin Books for Children, 2012.

Eye to Eye: How Animals See the World by Steve Jenkins. Boston: Houghton Mifflin Harcourt, 2014.

Art Project: Collage Animals

Think about some of your favorite animals. Maybe it is a cat or dog, an elephant or even an octopus. When you look at those animals, notice that they all have textures and a mixture of colors. Whether feathers, scales, or a combination of skin and fur, animals have a variety of textures and colors. Using an assortment of collected papers, create a collage over an animal shape or sketch.

PIECES NEEDED

- Nonfiction books with pictures of animals to get ideas
- White paper to trace animals from books, sketches of animals, or die-cut animals
- A variety of different papers (colorful magazines, old newspapers and books, scrapbook paper, construction paper, etc.)
- Glue
- Scissors
- Markers to add eyes and other details to collage if desired
- Table covers to protect tables as needed

DIRECTIONS

1. Decide which animal you would like to create. If tracing the animal from a book, place the white paper over the picture and outline, or try to sketch the animal yourself. If die-cut shapes are available, select the shape of your choice.
2. Looking at the animal, determine what papers should be used on different areas of the animal's body.
3. Cut or rip pieces of the chosen paper and fit them within your animal shape. If collage paper goes beyond the animal's outline, trim the paper around the animal when you are finished. Use a variety of papers and add depth and dimension to your animal.
4. Sign your work of art and display!

12

Wave

Charcoal and Pencil

Wave

Suzy Lee. San Francisco: Chronicle Books, 2008.
Suzy Lee's illustrations tell the story of a little girl playing at the beach and chasing the waves back into the ocean. Her bravado, however, is soon challenged as a wave comes crashing

down on her. *Wave* is a wordless book with all the sass of the girl, as well as her shock at the wave, evident in the illustrations.

ABOUT THE ILLUSTRATOR: Suzy Lee

Suzy Lee is best known for her wordless illustrated children's books. In 2016, Lee made the short list for the Hans Christian Andersen Award, the highest international honor given to children's book creators. Suzy Lee's ability to share her stories through simple pencil illustrations allows readers to use their imaginations to create the story. You can learn more about Suzy Lee at suzyleebooks.com.

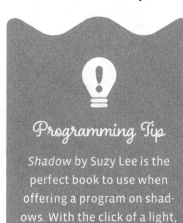

Programming Tip

Shadow by Suzy Lee is the perfect book to use when offering a program on shadows. With the click of a light, the shadow world comes to life. After reading the book, create your own shadow world for the children by making stick puppets and turning on lamps to cast shadows on the wall.

ABOUT THE TECHNIQUE: Charcoal and Pencil

Typically, there are three types of charcoal: compressed, vine, and pencil. Compressed charcoal is generally darker than vine charcoal, makes a darker mark, and is harder to smudge. Vine charcoal is softer and fills in your paper easily. Pencil charcoal comes in a range from hard to soft and can make very fine lines.

BOOKS TO DISPLAY

Lines by Suzy Lee. San Francisco: Chronicle Books, 2017.

Shadow by Suzy Lee. San Francisco: Chronicle Books, 2010.

This Beautiful Day by Richard Jackson and Suzy Lee. New York: Atheneum Books for Young Readers, 2017.

Art Project: Sketch with Charcoal

Think of a time when you were at the beach or pool. Maybe you were running through the sprinkler at a friend's house. Using pencils or charcoal, or both, re-create a fun summer memory.

PIECES NEEDED

- Charcoal drawing paper or construction paper
- Charcoal pencils
- Assorted colored pencils to add a splash of color if desired
- Table covers to protect tables as needed

DIRECTIONS

1. Think of a picture you would like to create.
2. Using a charcoal pencil, sketch your illustration. To add shading to your picture, use the side of the pencil to fill in the drawing. To get fine lines, use the point. To get darker lines and shadowing, press harder on the pencil.
3. Suzy Lee often selects one color to add to her illustrations. If there is a color that would enhance your picture, add it using a colored pencil.
4. Share the story behind your picture.
5. Sign your work of art and display!

13

The Red Book

The Red Book

Barbara Lehman. Boston: Houghton Mifflin, 2004.

What happens when two children, in two different places, find a red book? Magic! The red book provides a window to a child with another red book, allowing both children to experience a new world and find a friend.

ABOUT THE ILLUSTRATOR:
Barbara Lehman

Barbara Lehman is best known for her wordless picture books in which children are magically transported to other places. Before creating her picture books, Lehman creates a reference notebook filled with all the research she may need for the detailed illustrations. Lehman is the recipient of the Caldecott Honor award for *The Red Book* (2005). You can learn more about Barbara Lehman and see images of her work at barbaralehmanbooks.com.

Programming Tip

In *Museum Trip* by Barbara Lehman, a boy is on a field trip at a museum when he wanders into a labyrinth of adventures. Share this book before your next visit to a museum or science center to spark excitement about the upcoming trip.

ABOUT THE TECHNIQUE:
Ink, Watercolor, and Gouache

Watercolor is a type of paint mixed with water. By incorporating water, the paint colors can be diluted, creating lighter shades. Lehman draws her illustrations in ink first and then adds a watercolor wash. If she needs to create opaque lettering or details, Lehman uses gouache.

BOOKS TO DISPLAY

Museum Trip by Barbara Lehman. Boston: Houghton Mifflin Harcourt, 2006.

Red Again by Barbara Lehman. Boston: Houghton Mifflin Harcourt, 2017.

The Secret Box by Barbara Lehman. Boston: Houghton Mifflin Harcourt, 2011.

Art Project: Red Book

Use your imagination to create magic. Do you have a friend or relative who lives far away from you? Is there a special place you have visited that you would like to see again? Create your own red book with illustrations detailing where you would like to travel and how you would get there.

PIECES NEEDED
- Red construction paper (2 pieces)
- Watercolor paper (1 or 2 pieces)
- Pencil
- Ballpoint pen
- Watercolor paints
- Paintbrushes and plate for paint palette
- Water and paper towels for rinsing brushes
- Table covers to protect tables as needed

DIRECTIONS
1. Using pencil or ink, create an illustration on watercolor paper of where you would like to travel and another of how you would get there.
2. Add color to your illustrations with watercolor paints. The brush should not be too wet; you can always add more color if needed.
3. Make a cover for your book with the red construction paper.
4. When illustrations are dry, assemble the book.
5. Sign your book cover and display!

14

Duck for President

Ink and Watercolor

Duck for President

Doreen Cronin, pictures by Betsy Lewin. New York: Simon and Schuster Books for Young Readers, 2004.

Tired of his chores, Duck decides to hold an election so he can be in charge of the farm. But as Duck keeps winning elections—from being in charge of the farm to becoming president of the country—he learns that with great power comes more responsibilities. *Duck for President* is a fun, easy way to introduce children to the idea of elections and the political system.

ABOUT THE ILLUSTRATOR: Betsy Lewin

Betsy Lewin is best known for her illustrated children's books. Lewin is the recipient of the Caldecott Honor award for *Click, Clack, Moo: Cows That Type* (2001).

When not working, Lewin travels the world gathering mementos and inspiration for her books and illustrations. You can learn more about Betsy Lewin and see images of her work at betsylewin.com.

ABOUT THE TECHNIQUE:
Ink and Watercolor

Watercolor is a type of paint mixed with water. By incorporating water, the paint colors can be diluted, creating lighter shades. Lewin often draws her illustrations in ink first and then adds a watercolor wash.

Programming Tip

Many children have not seen a typewriter. Ask friends and family if they have a typewriter you can display during the program. Demonstrate how the typewriter works and have the children take turns typing.

BOOKS TO DISPLAY

Click, Clack, Moo: Cows That Type by Doreen Cronin, pictures by Betsy Lewin.
New York: Simon and Schuster Books for Young Readers, 2000.

Click, Clack, Peep! by Doreen Cronin and Betsy Lewin. New York: Atheneum
Books for Young Readers, 2015.

Click, Clack, Surprise! by Doreen Cronin and Betsy Lewin. New York: Atheneum
Books for Young Readers, 2016.

Art Project: Farm Illustration

Have you taken a ride in the country? Often there are rolling fields of green and
a bright red barn. Have you visited a farm or an orchard? Create a pencil or pen
illustration of a farm, then add watercolor paint.

PIECES NEEDED

- Light-colored watercolor paper or construction paper
- Pencil
- Watercolor paints
- Paintbrushes and plate for paint palette
- Water and paper towels for rinsing brushes
- Black marker or ink pen
- Table covers to protect tables as needed

DIRECTIONS

1. Using a pencil, sketch your farm. Possible additions to the farm include a
   barn, animals, vegetables, and trees.
2. Using a black marker or ink, draw over your sketch.
3. Using watercolor paints, add color to your illustration. The brush should not
   be too wet; you can always add more color if needed.
4. Sign your work of art and display!

15

Maybe Something Beautiful

Acrylics

Maybe Something Beautiful: How Art Transformed a Neighborhood

F. Isabel Campoy and Theresa Howell, illustrated by Rafael López. Boston: Houghton Mifflin Harcourt, 2016.

Mira lives in a gray city but loves to create art. When she passes out her drawings to her neighbors, a muralist sees the possibility of something beautiful. Soon the entire community comes together to paint vibrant murals throughout the neighborhood.

Programming Tip

Tito Puente, Mambo King by Monica Brown and Rafael López (New York: Rayo, 2013) introduces the music of Tito Puente, the King of Mambo, to children. By making simple music shakers with toilet paper rolls or folded paper plates and dried beans, children can create their own salsa rhythms. Combine with the titles in this chapter to create a Hispanic Heritage storytime.

ABOUT THE ILLUSTRATOR: Rafael López

Rafael López is best known for his bold illustrations in children's picture books, murals, commissioned postage stamps, and posters. *Maybe Something Beautiful* is inspired by the creation of the Urban Art Trail movement that López founded, reviving his community through art with murals. You can learn more about Rafael López and see images of his work at rafaellopez.com.

ABOUT THE TECHNIQUE: Acrylics

Acrylics are fast-drying paints that can be mixed with water to create lighter shades but that become water-resistant when dry. López often uses acrylics on wood surfaces to create his illustrations.

BOOKS TO DISPLAY

Book Fiesta! by Pat Mora, illustrated by Rafael López. New York: Rayo, an imprint of HarperCollins, 2009.

The Cazuela That the Farm Maiden Stirred by Samantha R. Vamos, illustrated by Rafael López. Watertown, MA: Charlesbridge, 2011.

Drum Dream Girl: How One Girl's Courage Changed Music by Margarita Engle and Rafael López. New York: Houghton Mifflin Harcourt, 2015.

Art Project: Mural Painting

Paint a mural to discover the joy of working together and building a sense of community. As a group, decide the theme for your mural.

PIECES NEEDED

- Bulletin board paper
- Pencil
- Acrylic paint
- Paintbrushes and plate for paint palette
- Water and paper towels for rinsing brushes
- Table covers to protect tables as needed

DIRECTIONS

1. Choose a theme for the mural—possibly a field of flowers and trees, or a sidewalk and city buildings.
2. With a pencil, sketch a design on the bulletin board paper for the children to paint, or divide the bulletin board paper into sections and have the children draw something on their section that they would like to paint.
3. Use acrylic paints to add color to the designs on the paper. The brush should not be too wet; you can always add more color if needed.
4. Have each child sign the mural and display!

Mama, Is It Summer Yet?

Cut Paper

Mama, Is It Summer Yet?

Nikki McClure. New York: Abrams Books for Young Readers, 2010.

A little boy is eager for summer to arrive and repeatedly asks, "Mama, is it summer yet?" Mama encourages the boy to look closely for signs of each season. Through cut paper illustrations, we experience the seasons changing and the joy of summer finally arriving.

ABOUT THE ILLUSTRATOR: Nikki McClure

Nikki McClure is best known for her cut paper illustrated picture books. Using an X-Acto knife and black paper, she cuts connected images to tell the story. While cutting, McClure decides the width of the line and what areas will be black or white in the illustration. When McClure is not creating picture books, she is working on her annual calendar. You can learn more about Nikki McClure and see images of her work at nikkimcclure.com.

ABOUT THE TECHNIQUE: Cut Paper

Cut paper art uses shapes cut from papers and arranged into compositions. Nikki McClure often uses a pencil to create the illustration on black paper and then uses an X-Acto knife to cut the paper, creating the outline and details of each image in the book. You can watch a video of her technique at youtube.com/watch?v=NRBGoraYG3M.

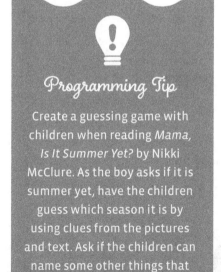

Programming Tip

Create a guessing game with children when reading *Mama, Is It Summer Yet?* by Nikki McClure. As the boy asks if it is summer yet, have the children guess which season it is by using clues from the pictures and text. Ask if the children can name some other things that can be found in each season.

BOOKS TO DISPLAY

In by Nikki McClure. New York: Abrams Appleseed, 2015.

To Market, to Market by Nikki McClure. New York: Abrams Books for Young
Readers, 2011.

Waiting for High Tide by Nikki McClure. New York: Abrams Books for Young
Readers, 2016.

Art Project: Cut Paper Scene

Cut paper projects allow you to showcase your imagination. Create a summer illustration using cut paper for image details such as flowers, trees, leaves, waves, the
sun, and more.

PIECES NEEDED

- Black construction paper
- Background construction paper in a color of your choice
- Scissors
- Colored pencils
- Glue

DIRECTIONS

1. Using scissors, cut images from black construction paper to create your summer scene.
2. Glue images to another piece of construction paper to create your illustration.
3. Add additional details and color with colored pencils as desired.
4. Sign your work of art and display!

Niño Wrestles the World

Mixed Media, Acrylics, and Inks

Niño Wrestles the World

Yuyi Morales. New York: Roaring Brook Press, 2013.

Lucha libre, or theatrical wrestling, is popular throughout Mexico and many other Central and South American countries. Yuyi Morales celebrates this aspect of pop culture as Niño's imagination takes him into the world of lucha libre, where he battles some of his most fearsome opponents, finally facing his twin sisters. Full of fun, *Niño Wrestles the World* appeals to children from any culture.

Programming Tip

Thunder Boy Jr. by Sherman Alexie, with vivid illustrations by Yuyi Morales, is a wonderful story. A little boy shares his father's name but expresses his desire to be his own person with his own name. The story expresses the need to find your own identity while honoring your cultural heritage. Bold illustrations depict the Native American traditions of the boy's people.

ABOUT THE ILLUSTRATOR:
Yuyi Morales

Yuyi Morales is best known for her children's picture books that feature an array of bold, dreamlike illustrations and varied artistic techniques. Although Morales often uses acrylics for her painted illustrations, she also makes dolls, marionettes, puppets, and props for her books. Morales is the recipient of the Caldecott Honor award for *Viva Frida* (2015). You can learn more about Yuyi Morales and see images of her work at yuyimorales.com.

ABOUT THE TECHNIQUE:
Mixed Media, Acrylics, and Inks

Acrylics are fast-drying paints that can be mixed with water to create lighter shades but that become water-resistant when dry. Ink is used to add details to the work.

BOOKS TO DISPLAY

Georgia in Hawaii: When Georgia O'Keeffe Painted What She Pleased by Amy Novesky, illustrated by Yuyi Morales. Boston: Houghton Mifflin Harcourt, 2012.

Thunder Boy Jr. by Sherman Alexie, illustrated by Yuyi Morales. New York: Little, Brown, 2016.

Viva Frida by Yuyi Morales. New York: Roaring Brook Press, 2014.

Art Project: Lucha Masks

Experience the fantasy of *lucha libre.* Wrestlers, called *luchadores,* often wear masks to hide their identity. Create your own mask and your own lucha libre story.

PIECES NEEDED

- Lucha libre mask template copied from Yuyi Morales's website (yuyimorales.com/nino_masks.html)
- Card stock to make copies of mask templates, or create your own mask template
- Acrylic paint
- Paintbrushes and plate for paint palette
- Water and paper towels for rinsing brushes
- Ballpoint pen or other ink pens
- Scissors
- Hole punch
- String
- Table covers to protect tables as needed

DIRECTIONS

1. Decide which mask you would like to make and have enough copies for each student. If you have card stock available, use it to make the copies of the templates.
2. Add acrylic paint to the mask. The brush should not be too wet; you can always add more color if needed.
3. Add details with ink if desired.
4. When the mask is dry, carefully cut the outline of the mask and eyes.
5. Punch holes in the sides of the mask and tie strings in the holes.
6. Sign your work of art and display!

18

The Three Billy Goats Gruff

The Three Billy Goats Gruff

Jerry Pinkney. New York: Little, Brown, 2017.

The Three Billy Goats are in search of rich, sweet grass, but in order to reach the grass they must face the Troll. In the retelling of this classic story, Jerry Pinkney adds a fish to threaten the Troll, just as the Troll had threatened the Billy Goats, allowing for a discussion about bullying and treatment of others.

ABOUT THE ILLUSTRATOR: Jerry Pinkney

Jerry Pinkney is best known for his illustrated children's books. Using few words and vivid watercolor illustrations, many of Pinkney's books retell fables and folktales, allowing readers to use their imagination to fill in the story. Pinkney is the recipient of the Caldecott Medal for the best illustrated children's book, *The Lion and the Mouse* (2010). He has also received Caldecott Honor awards for *Noah's Ark* (2003), *The Ugly Duckling* (2000), *John Henry* (1995), *The Talking Eggs: A Folktale from the American South* (1990), and *Mirandy and Brother Wind* (1989). You can learn more about Jerry Pinkney and see images of his work at jerrypinkneystudio.com.

ABOUT THE TECHNIQUE: Watercolor

Watercolor is a type of paint mixed with water. By incorporating water, the paint colors can be diluted, creating lighter shades.

Programming Tip

Folktales are stories passed down orally through generations. These stories often explain things that people do not understand, or they provide a lesson or moral for children. While sharing the folktales, make sure to discuss the lessons learned in the story.

BOOKS TO DISPLAY

The Grasshopper and the Ants by Jerry Pinkney. New York: Little, Brown, 2015.

The Lion and the Mouse by Jerry Pinkney. New York: Little, Brown, 2009.

The Tortoise and the Hare by Jerry Pinkney. New York: Little, Brown, 2013.

Art Project: Create a Troll

Trolls can be fun when you use this simple fold-and-press technique to make them. Think about what colors you want your troll to be and whether your troll will have a silly or happy expression.

PIECES NEEDED

- Shapes for eyes, nose, and mouth precut from colored construction paper
- Glue
- Construction paper in various colors
- Paint (any kids' paint will work well)
- Table covers to protect tables as needed

DIRECTIONS

1. Fold construction paper in half, then reopen to full size.
2. Place drops of paint randomly on one side of the construction paper and in the center of the paper. Be careful not to get paint too close to the edge of the paper or the paint will ooze out. Use a variety of colors.
3. Carefully fold the unpainted portion of the construction paper over the painted portion.
4. Apply pressure to the folded paper and squeeze paint drops around so there is a design on both sides of the paper when unfolded.
5. When the paint is dry, glue on shapes to create the details of the troll's face.
6. Sign your work of art and display!

We Came to America

We Came to America

Faith Ringgold. New York: Alfred A. Knopf, 2016.

We Came to America celebrates the diverse cultures of America through vibrant illustrations in the story quilt folk tradition. Each immigrant group has its own individual story and identity, but together immigrants make up the patchwork of our United States. With a look at the cultures and gifts immigrants have brought with them, *We Came to America* reminds us that together we make our country great.

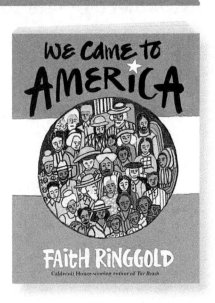

ABOUT THE ILLUSTRATOR: Faith Ringgold

Faith Ringgold's best-known artwork includes paintings, story quilts, sculptures, and children's books. Ringgold is the recipient of the Coretta Scott King award and the Caldecott Honor award for *Tar Beach* (1991). While in Amsterdam she was inspired by Tibetan tankas (paintings framed in cloth) and began creating a series of story quilts with images set in the context of African American history. You can learn more about Faith Ringgold and see images of her work at faithringgold.com.

ABOUT THE TECHNIQUE: Story Quilts

Story quilts use scraps of fabric or painted fabric to create a picture that tells a story. Slaves brought appliqué and other quilting techniques to the United States from Africa. Often quilts can feature one motif repeated, such as birds, leaves, and the like. Faith Ringgold expands this process to create stories she wants to tell. Using strong colors and bold designs, Ringgold creates a social commentary on history, events, and pop culture.

Programming Tip

Quilting is an art form brought to the United States by African slaves. Share this project during Black History Month to enhance related programming.

BOOKS TO DISPLAY

Aunt Harriet's Underground Railroad in the Sky by Faith Ringgold. New York: Crown, 1992.

Harlem Renaissance Party by Faith Ringgold. New York: Amistad, an imprint of HarperCollins, 2015.

Tar Beach by Faith Ringgold. New York: Crown, 1991.

Art Project: Create Your Own Story Quilt

Think of a vacation memory or a moment in time when you were very happy. Perhaps you were at the beach or mountains with your family or, possibly, learning to ride a bike or swim with a parent. Maybe you went to a special party. Is there a person, place, or thing you especially like and want to remember? Create a picture depicting that special memory and then add a border with assorted fabric or scrapbook squares.

PIECES NEEDED

- Two sizes of paper (you will draw the memory on the smaller piece of paper and glue it in the center of the larger paper)
- Crayons, colored pencils, markers, paints, and other decorating items
- Glue
- Scrapbook paper or fabric cut into squares
- Table covers to protect tables as needed

DIRECTIONS

1. Create a colorful memory on the smaller piece of paper.
2. Glue your memory drawing onto the center of the larger paper.
3. Using assorted colors and patterns of scrapbook paper or fabric, create a border around your memory picture.
4. Sign your work of art and display!

20

I'm the Biggest Thing in the Ocean

Mixed Media—Watercolor, Cut Paper, and Ink

I'm the Biggest Thing in the Ocean

Kevin Sherry. New York: Dial Books for Young Readers, 2007.

One giant squid is sure he is the biggest thing in the ocean—until he discovers a whale. In *I'm the Biggest Thing in the Ocean*, Kevin Sherry explores many deep-sea animals and their relative sizes, while a giant squid learns that believing you're the biggest depends on who you're swimming with. Bold illustrations and simple text make this a wonderful picture book for any age.

Programming Tip

Teach children the value of working together by creating an ocean mural with the group. On a large piece of white bulletin board paper, have the children paint a watercolor ocean. While the watercolor layer is drying, have the children cut out different sea animals from construction paper. After gluing on the sea animals, the children can add details with black ink pens or markers. Have each child sign the mural.

ABOUT THE ILLUSTRATOR: Kevin Sherry

Kevin Sherry is best known for his illustrated children's books and his juvenile fiction books that feature graphic novel-style illustrations. In addition to writing and illustrating books, Sherry is a puppeteer and makes all his own puppets. He performs puppet shows for adults and children. You can learn more about Kevin Sherry and see images of his work at kevinsherryonline.com.

ABOUT THE TECHNIQUE: Mixed Media—Watercolor, Cut Paper, and Ink

Kevin Sherry completes his illustrations in layers, each using a different technique. The background is created with watercolor. Cut paper shapes create the animals and objects. Ink adds the final details to the illustrations.

BOOKS TO DISPLAY

Acorns Everywhere! by Kevin Sherry. New York: Dial Books for Young Readers, 2009.

I'm the Best Artist in the Ocean by Kevin Sherry. New York: Dial Books for Young Readers, 2008.

Turtle Island by Kevin Sherry. New York: Dial Books for Young Readers, 2014.

Art Project: Ocean Illustration

Create your own ocean illustration. By using watercolors to paint the water, the sea will look like it is swirling and flowing. Then glue some of your favorite sea creatures onto the paper, adding details with a black marker or pen.

PIECES NEEDED
- Light-colored watercolor paper or construction paper for the background
- Construction paper in an assortment of colors
- Scissors
- Glue
- Watercolor paints
- Paintbrushes and plate for paint palette
- Water and paper towels for rinsing brushes
- Black marker or ink pen
- Table covers to protect tables as needed

DIRECTIONS
1. Using watercolor paints, create an ocean background on watercolor paper or construction paper. The brush should not be too wet; you can always add more color if needed.
2. While the paper is drying, cut sea animals from the construction paper in a variety of colors.
3. When the ocean paper is dry, glue the sea animals onto the paper.
4. Add details to your sea creatures with a marker or pen.
5. Sign your work of art and display!

21

A Perfect Day

A Perfect Day

Lane Smith. New York: Roaring Brook Press, 2017.

Today is a perfect day in Bert's backyard. The cat, dog, chickadee, and squirrel are all happily enjoying the day—that is, until bear arrives; now it is just a perfect day for him! Lane Smith's textured illustrations demonstrate each animal's joy of the day.

ABOUT THE ILLUSTRATOR: Lane Smith

Lane Smith is best known for his illustrated children's books. Prior to becoming a children's book illustrator and author, he worked as a freelance illustrator for many magazines. Smith is the recipient of the Caldecott Honor award for *Grandpa Green* (2012) and *The Stinky Cheese Man and Other Fairly Stupid Tales* (1993). You can learn more about Lane Smith and see images of his work at lanesmithbooks.com.

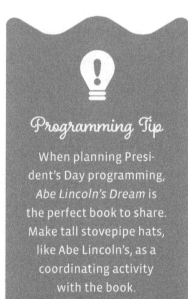

Programming Tip

When planning President's Day programming, *Abe Lincoln's Dream* is the perfect book to share. Make tall stovepipe hats, like Abe Lincoln's, as a coordinating activity with the book.

ABOUT THE TECHNIQUE: Mixed Media

Mixed media is art created with more than one medium. Lane Smith uses oils, pencils, pen and ink, collage, watercolor, and other items that he feels are needed for the book. Often he uses oil paint on board, building up several thin layers of the oil paint, sealing each layer with acrylic spray varnish. This process causes a chemical reaction to occur between the oil paint and the acrylic varnish, creating the dots of color and texture found in many of his books.

BOOKS TO DISPLAY

Abe Lincoln's Dream by Lane Smith. New York: Roaring Brook Press, 2012.

Grandpa Green by Lane Smith. New York: Roaring Brook Press, 2011.

There Is a Tribe of Kids by Lane Smith. New York: Roaring Brook Press, 2016.

Art Project: Perfect Day Texture

What is your perfect day? Create a picture of your perfect day using a variety of items to paint and create texture.

PIECES NEEDED

- Watercolor or construction paper
- Paint (acrylic, watercolor, or any other children's paint)
- Paintbrushes and plate for paint palette
- Assorted items to paint with (cotton swabs, plastic forks, erasers, sponges, etc.)
- Water and paper towels for rinsing brushes
- Table covers to protect tables as needed

DIRECTIONS

1. Think of what you would like to create for your perfect day—or maybe your pet's perfect day.
2. Paint your perfect day with the assorted items available to create a variety of textures. What creates soft fluffy textures, or sharp spikey ones? If you have clouds, try painting them with a cotton swab, or use a fork for blades of grass.
3. Sign your work of art and display!

Because Amelia Smiled

Mixed Media

Because Amelia Smiled

David Ezra Stein. Somerville, MA: Candlewick Press, 2012.

The ripple effect of kindness is demonstrated in the picture book *Because Amelia Smiled*. Amelia smiles as she skips down the street, inspiring her neighbor to send a package to her grandson, which in turn makes her grandson happy and inspires him too. As these acts of kindness are shared around the world, we are reminded that it all can start with us.

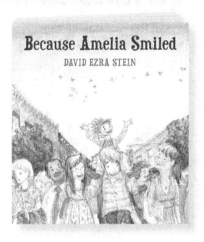

ABOUT THE ILLUSTRATOR: David Ezra Stein

David Ezra Stein is best known for his mixed media illustrated children's books. He began creating stories as a child and often left drawings on sticky note pads around the house. Stein is the recipient of the Caldecott Honor award for *Interrupting Chicken* (2011). You can learn more about David Ezra Stein and see images of his work at davidezrastein.com.

Programming Tip

Interrupting Chicken by David Ezra Stein is the story of Little Red Chicken, who constantly interrupts Papa while he tells her bedtime stories. Papa's solution is to suggest that Little Red tell him a bedtime story instead. After reading this book, invite the children to share their own bedtime stories and create their own picture book.

ABOUT THE TECHNIQUE: Mixed Media

Mixed media art is created by using more than one medium. David Ezra Stein often uses watercolor, crayon, and Uni-ball pens for his illustrations. He has also created a technique that he calls "Stein-lining," a process in which crayon is rubbed on label paper, the label paper is turned over onto drawing paper, then a pen is used to draw on the backside of the label paper to create a crayon image on the drawing paper. A demonstration of "Stein-lining" can be seen at youtube.com/watch?v=-WKlw9TabKU.

BOOKS TO DISPLAY

Ice Boy by David Ezra Stein. Somerville, MA: Candlewick Press, 2017.

I'm My Own Dog by David Ezra Stein. Somerville, MA: Candlewick Press, 2014.

Interrupting Chicken by David Ezra Stein. Somerville, MA: Candlewick Press, 2010.

Art Project: "Stein-lining"

Acts of kindness make us happier and make the world a nicer place. Think of something that makes you happy—possibly a rainbow, an animal, or maybe a flower. Use "Stein-lining" to create a picture of something that makes you happy and then share your picture with a special friend or family member.

PIECES NEEDED

- Label or parchment paper (Parchment paper is inexpensive and can be purchased in large rolls without wasting labels. You can achieve the same effect by using parchment paper.)
- Light-colored construction or drawing paper
- Crayons
- Masking tape
- Ballpoint pens
- Watercolor paints
- Colored pencils
- Paintbrushes and plate for paint palette
- Water and paper towels for rinsing brushes
- Table covers to protect tables as needed

DIRECTIONS

1. Thickly cover the shiny side of the parchment paper with crayon rubbings.
2. Turn the parchment paper over onto the drawing paper. Tape the corners in place if you are concerned that the paper may shift while you are drawing the picture.
3. Using a ballpoint pen, draw a picture of something that makes you happy.
4. Carefully remove the parchment paper when you've finished. There should be a colorful image left on the drawing paper.
5. Enhance your picture with watercolor paints, crayons, or colored pencils.
6. Sign your work of art and display!

23
Daddy Hugs

Daddy Hugs

Nancy Tafuri. New York: Little, Brown, 2015.
Daddy hugs are the very best! Baby animals
and children are shown cuddling for a special
moment with dad. Nancy Tafuri's simple text
and watercolor illustrations bring to life the
quiet moments shared by families.

ABOUT THE ILLUSTRATOR: Nancy Tafuri

Nancy Tafuri is best known for her watercolor
and pencil illustrations in children's books. Tafuri is the recipient of the Caldecott
Honor award for *Have You Seen My Duckling?* (1985). Tafuri has always loved animals,
and her detailed illustrations often feature woodland animals in their natural
habitat. You can learn more about Nancy Tafuri and see images of her work at
nancytafuri.com.

Programming Tip

Nancy Tafuri's *What the Sun
Sees, What the Moon Sees* (New
York: Greenwillow Books, 1997) is
the perfect book to share when
discussing day and night. After
reading the book, discuss things
found in the day and the night.
Create your own daytime and
nighttime book using pictures
cut from magazines and then
glued to construction paper.

ABOUT THE TECHNIQUE: Watercolor Pencil

Watercolor is a type of paint mixed with
water. By incorporating water, the paint
colors can be diluted, creating lighter
shades. Watercolor pencils are used
in multiple ways. Color an area with a
pencil, then dip a brush in clean water
and brush over the drawing to create a
watercolor wash effect. Draw on damp
paper to create color that spreads and
blends easily. Dip a pencil into water to
create fluid strokes of vivid color.

BOOKS TO DISPLAY

All Kinds of Kisses by Nancy Tafuri. New York: Little, Brown, 2012.

The Busy Little Squirrel by Nancy Tafuri. New York: Simon and Schuster Books for Young Readers, 2006.

Goodnight, My Duckling by Nancy Tafuri. New York: Scholastic, 2005.

Art Project: Watercolor Pencil Animals

Using one of the drawings provided, or a design of your choice, create a watercolor painting with watercolor pencils. Experiment with drawing and creating a watercolor finish on your illustration of an animal. The pencils will allow you to add more details, such as hair, fur, and scales.

PIECES NEEDED

- An assortment of images to paint (some suggestions to get started are provided)
- Pencil
- Watercolor pencils
- Paintbrushes
- Water and paper towels for rinsing brushes
- Table covers to protect tables as needed

DIRECTIONS

1. Decide which picture you would like to create and make enough copies for each student. If you have watercolor paper available, use it to make the copies of the picture.
2. Using watercolor pencil, add color to your illustration. Try different ways of using your watercolor pencils as described in the About the Technique section.
3. Sign your work of art and display!

24

Tuesday

Tuesday

David Wiesner. New York: Clarion Books, 1991.

Normally there is nothing unusual about a Tuesday night, but in David Wiesner's fantastic and nearly wordless picture book, *Tuesday,* things are a bit strange. Lily pads with frogs upon them lift into the night sky, zooming past birds and clotheslines. As the sun comes up the lily pads fall down, leaving the frogs to scatter and the police to wonder why lily pads are in the streets.

ABOUT THE ILLUSTRATOR: David Wiesner

David Wiesner is best known for his illustrated children's books that often feature a bit of fantasy and vivid imagination. Wiesner is the recipient of the Caldecott Medal for best illustrated children's book for *Tuesday* (1992), *The Three Pigs* (2002), and *Flotsam* (2007). He has also received three Caldecott Honor awards for *Free Fall* (1989), *Sector 7* (2000), and *Mr. Wuffles!* (2015). Wiesner's ability to share stories through his inspired illustrations and use of very few, if any, words allows readers to use their imagination. You can learn more about David Wiesner and see images of his work at davidwiesner.com.

ABOUT THE TECHNIQUE: Watercolor

Watercolor is a type of paint mixed with water. By incorporating water, the paint colors can be diluted, creating lighter shades.

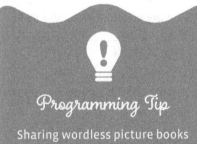

Programming Tip

Sharing wordless picture books presents a perfect opportunity to increase participation by children. Encourage discussion by asking clarifying questions about what they see and, at the end of the book, ask them to retell the story. Children will learn about story structure and sequencing as well as practice comprehension skills.

BOOKS TO DISPLAY

Art and Max by David Wiesner. Boston: Clarion Books, 2010.

Flotsam by David Wiesner. New York: Clarion Books, 2006.

Mr. Wuffles! by David Wiesner. New York: Clarion Books, Houghton Mifflin Harcourt, 2013.

Art Project: Wordless Story

Can you tell a story with only pictures? Think of a story you would like to tell and what illustrations you would create to tell the story if there were no words. Some ideas for stories could be an ocean wave crashing onto the shore, snowballs being rolled to make a snowperson, or a bird flying to a treetop.

PIECES NEEDED

- Construction paper (8½ by 11 inches) in a light color, folded in half. Children can create a four-page book with one piece of paper, or an eight-page book with two pieces of paper.
- Pencil
- Colored pencils
- Watercolor paints
- Paintbrushes and plate for paint palette
- Crayons
- Water and paper towels for rinsing brushes
- Table covers to protect tables as needed

DIRECTIONS

1. Think of the story you want to create and how many pictures you will need to tell the story. Remember, the front page will be the front cover of your book and the back page will be the back cover.
2. Using a pencil, sketch your illustrations.
3. Choose crayons, colored pencils, or watercolor paints to add color to your illustrations.
4. Sign your book on the cover page!

25

Don't Let the Pigeon Drive the Bus!

Cartoon

Don't Let the Pigeon Drive the Bus!

Mo Willems. New York: Hyperion Books for Children, 2003.

After the reader is asked to make sure the pigeon does not drive the bus, the very persistent pigeon repeatedly requests to drive the bus. Trying every trick known to a pigeon, he finally gives up asking when the driver returns to the bus, but a new vehicle quickly captures his interest. Simple text and illustrations, along with cartoonlike panels, tell this story that people of all ages adore.

ABOUT THE ILLUSTRATOR: Mo Willems

Mo Willems is best known for his illustrated children's books, including his series featuring Pigeon, Elephant and Piggie, and Knuffle Bunny. Willems began his career as a writer and animator for *Sesame Street* where he worked for nine seasons before publishing children's books. Willems is the recipient of Caldecott Honor awards for *Don't Let the Pigeon Drive the Bus!* (2004), *Knuffle Bunny: A Cautionary Tale* (2005), and *Knuffle Bunny Too: A Case of Mistaken Identity* (2008). You can learn more about Mo Willems and see images of his work at mowillems.com.

ABOUT THE TECHNIQUE: Cartoon

Cartoons are simplistic, one-dimensional drawings, often in sequential order telling a story. Willems's series of books are intentionally drawn simplistically so that characters can be reasonably copied by children.

Programming Tip

Mo Willems's website has an assortment of downloadable guides and kits. Make use of this excellent resource when planning activities for children (**pigeonpresents .com/get-busy**).

BOOKS TO DISPLAY

Knuffle Bunny: A Cautionary Tale by Mo Willems. New York: Hyperion Books for Children, 2004.

Sam, the Most Scaredy-Cat Kid in the Whole World by Mo Willems. New York: Disney-Hyperion, 2017.

The Thank You Book by Mo Willems. New York: Hyperion Books for Children, 2016.

Art Project: Create a Cartoon

Creating a story in cartoon form is fun and easy. Using the panels provided on the following page, think of a story you would like to share. Add illustrations to tell the story and a few words to express the characters' feelings or actions.

PIECES NEEDED
- Cartoon panels
- Card stock
- Pencil
- Crayons
- Colored pencils

DIRECTIONS
1. Using the panels provided, make enough copies for each student. If you have card stock available, use it to make the copies.
2. Using a pencil, add illustrations to each panel of the cartoon to move the story forward.
3. Use colored pencils or crayons to color the illustrations and add words to the panels.
4. Sign your work of art and display!

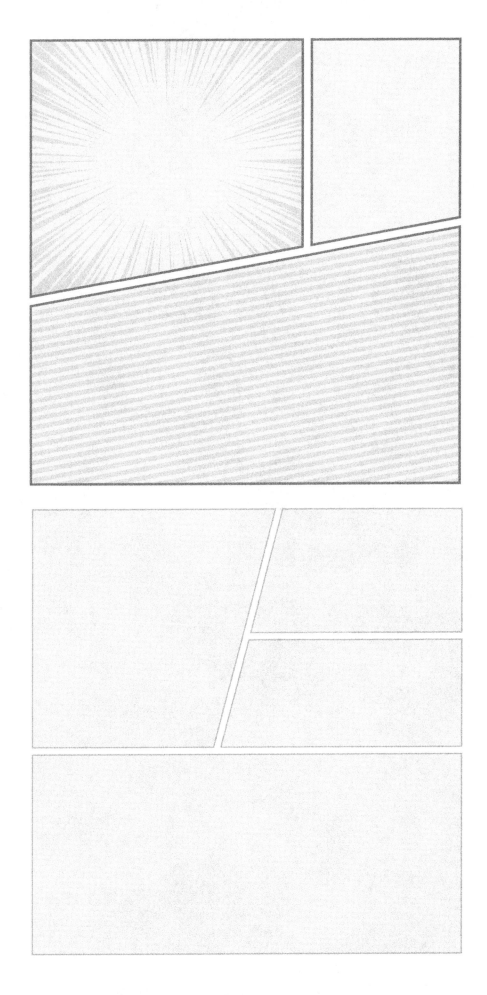

appendix
Materials Guidelines

ACRYLICS Acrylics are fast-drying paints that can be mixed with water to create lighter shades but that become water-resistant when dry.

CARTOONS Cartoons are simplistic, one-dimensional drawings, often in sequential order telling a story.

CHALK PASTELS Chalk pastels make soft marks and are easy to blend. They work well on thick, textured paper.

CHARCOAL Charcoal comes in different thicknesses and creates fluid marks. The side of a charcoal stick can cover large areas, while the end of the charcoal stick creates more controlled lines. Typically, there are three types of charcoal—compressed, vine, and pencil. Compressed charcoal is generally darker than vine charcoal, makes a darker mark, and is harder to smudge. Vine charcoal is softer and fills in your paper easily. Pencil charcoal comes in a range from hard to soft and can make very fine lines.

COLLAGE A collage is a work of art composed by pasting on a single surface various materials not normally associated with one another, such as newspaper clippings, parts of photographs, theater tickets, and fragments of an envelope.

COLORED PENCILS Colored pencils are soft-cored pencils in a variety of colors. The pencil's sharpness, the amount of pressure you apply, and the way you hold the pencil will affect the marks it makes.

GOUACHE PAINT   Gouache paint is similar to watercolor paint, although the color is opaque, or not able to be seen through, unlike watercolor, which is transparent.

GRAPHITE   Graphite sticks come in two thicknesses, that of a pencil or a crayon. Graphite is similar to a pencil but without the surrounding wood.

MIXED MEDIA   Mixed media art is created by using more than one medium.

OIL PAINT   Oil paint is slow-drying paint that contains oil.

OIL PASTELS   Oil pastels are used to create vivid color, especially when you apply pressure.

PENCILS   Pencils are common drawing tools that generally make a gray, uniform mark. Drawing pencils vary in hardness and blackness. The pencil's sharpness, the amount of pressure you apply, and the way you hold the pencil will affect the marks it makes.

PULP PAPERMAKING   In pulp papermaking, a fiber material is mixed with water to create a slurry. The wet fiber slurry is poured through stencils onto a draining screen and then allowed to dry. This process creates an image set within the paper.

WATERCOLOR   Watercolor is a type of paint mixed with water. By incorporating water, the paint colors can be diluted, creating lighter shades. It is best to start with a damp brush because using too much water can saturate the paper.

WATERCOLOR PAPER   Watercolor paper is often used when painting with watercolors because the specialty paper can absorb a lot of water without warping or causing the colors to bleed.

WATERCOLOR PENCILS   Watercolor pencils are used in multiple ways. Color an area with a watercolor pencil, then dip a brush in clean water and brush over the drawing to create a watercolor wash effect. Draw on damp paper to create color that spreads and blends easily. Dip a pencil into water to create fluid strokes of vivid color.

CPSIA information can be obtained
at www.ICGtesting.com
Printed in the USA
LVHW020351140622
721151LV00007B/593